AMAZING
ANIMAL FACTS

Written by Jacqui Bailey

DK Publishing

LONDON, NEW YORK,
MELBOURNE, MUNICH, AND DELHI

Editors   Joe Elliot and Jayne Miller
Senior Designer   Adrienne Hutchinson
Project Editor   Clare Lister
Production   Rochelle Talary
Managing Editor   Camilla Hallinan
Managing Art Editor   Sophia Tampakopoulos
Category Publisher   Sue Grabham

First American Edition, 2003

Published in the United States by
DK Publishing, Inc.
375 Hudson Street
New York, New York 10014

03 04 05 06 07 08 10 9 8 7 6 5 4 3 2 1

A Cataloging-in-Publication record for this book is available
from the Library of Congress.

ISBN 0-7894-9870-7

Reproduced in Singapore by Colourscan

Printed and bound in Hong Kong by Toppan

See our complete product line at
www.dk.com

CONTENTS

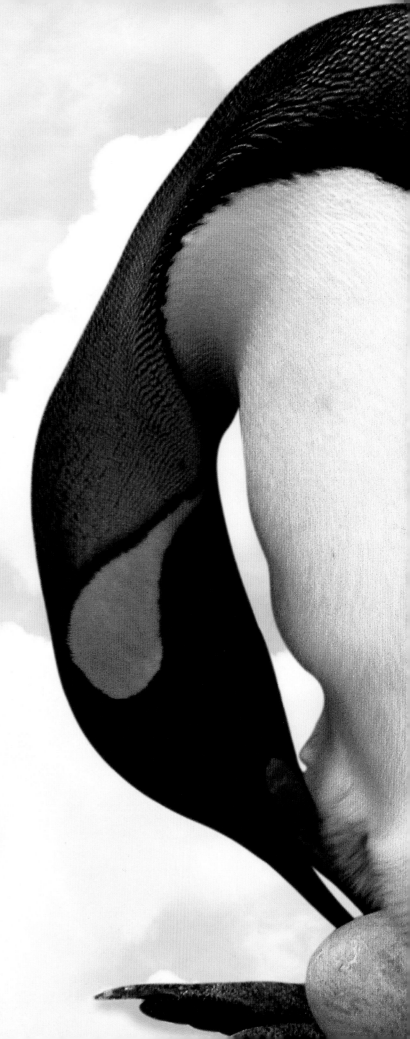

MAMMALS

Who's the biggest?

Mammals break all the records for largest, longest, and heaviest animals on land and in the oceans. The biggest land animals are African elephants, which can grow to 13 ft (4 m) tall and weigh over 6½ tons (6 metric tons)—that's over twice as tall as a human and as heavy as six cars. The biggest animal the world has ever known is the ocean-going blue whale—it can grow to 100 ft (30 m) long and weigh 175 tons (160 metric tons), which is six times as long and 25 times as heavy as an elephant.

Asian elephant

Q A Why are elephants in danger?

Elephants are too big to be hunted by most other animals, but humans kill them for their tusks. Tusks are the elephant's front teeth and are made of a highly prized material called ivory. To try to protect elephants, buying and selling ivory has been banned in many countries.

Elephant tusk

Q A When are two legs better than four?

Bears have four legs but will rear up and walk on their two hind legs to look at their surroundings or to make themselves look bigger when they are frightened. Gorillas, chimpanzees, and other apes can stand up and walk a few steps on two legs—but most of the time they use their arms, too.

Brown bear

Q A Which giant is the toughest?

Rhinoceroses have very tough skin. It is about ³/₄ in (2 cm) thick and covers their bodies like armor. Not even the claws of a big cat can tear it. When threatened, rhinos aim their horns at their attacker and charge head-on—racing at speeds up to 28 mph (45 km/h).

African rhinoceros

Round, flat feet spread out to carry the elephant's vast weight

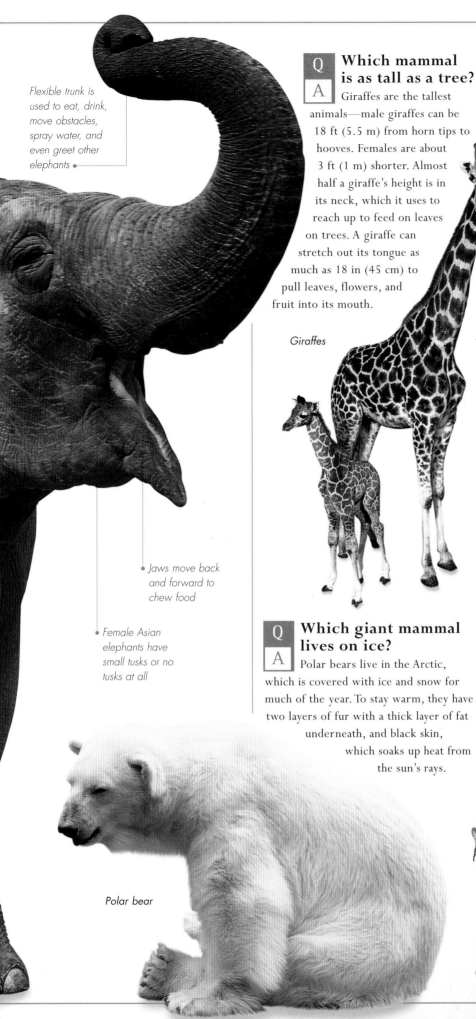

Flexible trunk is used to eat, drink, move obstacles, spray water, and even greet other elephants •

• *Jaws move back and forward to chew food*

• *Female Asian elephants have small tusks or no tusks at all*

Polar bear

Q
A | **Which mammal is as tall as a tree?**

Giraffes are the tallest animals—male giraffes can be 18 ft (5.5 m) from horn tips to hooves. Females are about 3 ft (1 m) shorter. Almost half a giraffe's height is in its neck, which it uses to reach up to feed on leaves on trees. A giraffe can stretch out its tongue as much as 18 in (45 cm) to pull leaves, flowers, and fruit into its mouth.

Giraffes

Q | A | **Which giant mammal lives on ice?**

Polar bears live in the Arctic, which is covered with ice and snow for much of the year. To stay warm, they have two layers of fur with a thick layer of fat underneath, and black skin, which soaks up heat from the sun's rays.

Q | A | **Which are the gentlest giants?**

In spite of their fierce reputation, gorillas are surprisingly gentle animals. They are mostly peaceful vegetarians, but they do eat a few insects and worms. The white-haired "silverback" male leader will sometimes beat his chest in warning, then charge and fight, but only when he is challenged or his family group is in danger.

Silverback male gorilla

More Facts

■ Elephant babies take 22 months to develop inside their mothers before they are born.

■ An elephant's trunk is really a very long nose with soft grippers on the end. There aren't any bones inside it, but there are about 100,000 muscles.

■ Rhinos can't see well, so they attack anything that looks like a threat—often charging straight into trees and rocks.

■ Giant pandas are the only bears that don't eat meat. They eat bamboo, a tough kind of grass.

■ Gorillas and chimpanzees are humans' closest cousins in the animal world.

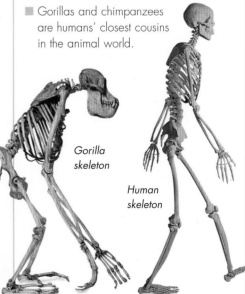

Gorilla skeleton

Human skeleton

Is smaller better?

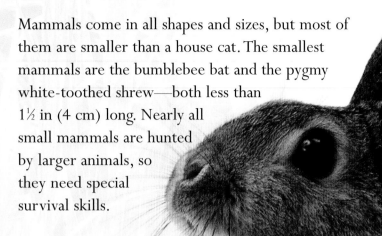

Mammals come in all shapes and sizes, but most of them are smaller than a house cat. The smallest mammals are the bumblebee bat and the pygmy white-toothed shrew—both less than 1½ in (4 cm) long. Nearly all small mammals are hunted by larger animals, so they need special survival skills.

Cottontail rabbit

Very flexible neck means that a rabbit can look almost directly behind it

Long, strong back legs help the rabbit to bound away from its attackers

Q A ### Who has teeth that never stop growing?

Squirrels, beavers, mice, hamsters, chipmunks, and rats—they all belong to a group of mammals known as rodents. Rodents have two large front teeth in each jaw for gnawing at tough woody stems, nuts, or anything else. The teeth are always growing because they are continuously being worn away.

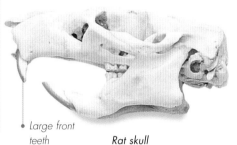

Large front teeth

Rat skull

Q A ### Who has the most dangerous smile?

When a monkey stares at you or opens its mouth wide and shows its teeth, it isn't making friends—it is threatening to attack. Monkeys make faces and screech or howl to show their feelings or warn each other. When a monkey wants to say hello, it smacks its lips together.

Short, strong front legs with 5 clawed toes on each foot for digging underground burrows

How do kittens become cats?

A kitten is born blind and helpless, and it stays close to its mother for protection. In just nine weeks, it will grow big enough to leave its mother and take care of itself.

1 A newborn kitten can't raise its head or walk. Its eyes and ears are closed, but it can smell.

House mice

Which mammals pack "snack boxes"?

Chipmunks do. Small bodies lose heat faster than large ones, so small mammals have to eat nearly all the time to keep warm. Chipmunks and some other rodents solve this problem by filling pockets in their cheeks with food for an extra between-meal snack.

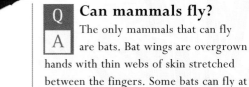

Borneo fruit bat, or flying fox

Which mammal has the most offspring?

Mice and rats breed at a rapid rate. Female house mice start to breed when they are 6 weeks old and can have up to 10 litters a year, with 5–7 babies in each litter. Most house mice are killed by traps or other animals—if they weren't, we would all be knee-deep in mice.

Chipmunk

Can mammals fly?

The only mammals that can fly are bats. Bat wings are overgrown hands with thin webs of skin stretched between the fingers. Some bats can fly at speeds of more than 30 mph (50 km/h). The largest bat is the flying fox. Its wings are about 3 ft (1 m) across.

Which is the deadliest mammal in history?

Rats can carry fleas and germs so deadly they can kill humans. Over 300 years ago, rat fleas spread a disease called the bubonic plague, or the Black Death, which killed millions of people.

Which mammals are the best acrobats?

Monkeys are excellent climbers, and most live in thick forests, where they can escape from hunters by leaping from branch to branch. They have hands with long fingers and thumbs (like humans) that are excellent for gripping, and most have long tails for balancing or holding on. Capuchin monkeys can also use simple tools—they hit nuts with stones to crack them.

Capuchin monkey

Brown rat

2 At 21 days old, the kitten can see, hear, mew, and raise its head, but it still cannot walk. Its first, or milk, teeth are through.

3 At 30 days old, the kitten can walk and likes exploring. It lives on solid food as well as its mother's milk.

4 At 63 days old, the kitten has given up milk. It plays games to practice hunting.

Are mammals fierce?

Meat-eating mammals, or carnivores, are among the most ferocious animals on land, and the fiercest of all are wild dogs and the big cats—lions, tigers, jaguars, leopards, and snow leopards. Mammal hunters have excellent sight and smell for tracking down their prey, speed and strength for catching it, and sharp claws and teeth for killing and for cutting into flesh.

Bengal tiger

Black leopard

Q A Which big cats are the biggest?

The largest and heaviest of all big cats are tigers. Tigers grow up to 9¼ ft (2.8 m) long—about six times as long as a house cat—and can weigh up to 660 lb (300 kg)—nearly as much as four men. They eat mostly deer and wild pigs but sometimes attack young elephants.

Red fox cubs

Q A When is a panther not a panther?

The black panther is really a type of leopard. Leopards usually have golden fur with black patches and spots—black leopards have the same dark patches, but they are hidden against an almost black background. Black leopards belong to normal leopard families, and their brothers and sisters have ordinary golden coats. Real panthers, also called pumas, cougars, or mountain lions, have clear brown fur with no patches or spots at all.

Q A Who are the leaders of the pack?

Gray wolves are the largest of all the wild dogs and are strong and clever hunters. They live and hunt in packs of up to 20, and each animal has a different level of importance in the pack. Only the leading male and female wolves mate and have young. Wolves can only run fast in short bursts, so they tire their prey by loping (running slowly) for hours.

Q A Why do fox cubs fight each other?

Young foxes learn their hunting skills by play-fighting with each other. Their rough games also establish a pecking order— the strongest foxes are feared and the weakest ones are picked on. Most foxes hunt on their own, using their excellent hearing to track small animals such as mice and even earthworms. They can also jump up to 3 ft (1 m) into the air to catch prey.

Gray wolves

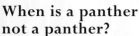

More Facts

■ A lion needs to eat 11–15 lb (5–7 kg) of meat every day—enough food for 25 people.

■ Cheetahs are the fastest animals on land. They can run at over 62 mph (100 km/h)—three times as fast as the fastest human runner.

■ After chasing and killing prey, it takes a cheetah half an hour to catch its breath before it can eat.

■ Only lions, jaguars, leopards, and tigers can roar. Their special voice boxes make incredibly loud and deep sounds—a male lion's roar can be heard up to 5 miles (8 km) away.

■ Big cats pull in their claws when they walk or run, but dogs can't—so you can tell their paw prints apart easily.

Cheetah

Q A Which lion does the most hunting?

Female lions do most of the hunting, and hunt in groups so they can kill animals much bigger than themselves. A male lion's job is to defend the pride, and although he doesn't hunt, the females will let him eat first.

4 large killing teeth

Thick mane for protecting head and neck

5 sharp claws on each foot are pulled in when not needed

Adult male lion

Muscled body weighs about 400 lb (180 kg), one-and-a-half times as heavy as a lioness

Who has long legs?

One way of staying out of trouble is to outrun it, and a number of mammal plant-eaters, or herbivores, do just that. Their long legs and ability to run great distances to escape danger have helped them to spread over most of the land areas of the world. They include deer, cattle, camels, and horses—the most successful long-distance runners of all. Horses and people have lived and worked together for more than 4,000 years, and horses are found almost everywhere there are humans.

Q | How do horses run so fast?

A With large lungs and long legs that let them take big strides, horses are built for speed. Their long, slim bones are attached to each other by strong, stretchy cords called ligaments that let the joints move very easily. Their joints are worked by strong muscles that keep a horse going over long distances and give it the power to jump fences and carry heavy loads.

Horse height is measured in "hands," from shoulder to ground. One hand is about 4 in (10 cm)

Dapple-gray mare cantering

Long jaws contain rows of grinding teeth to chew grass

Hoof made of keratin, the same stuff as human fingernails

Hind legs bend back for powerful, forward-springing steps

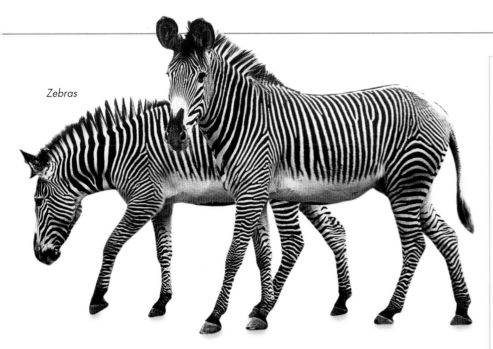

Zebras

More Facts

■ The biggest horses are Shire horses. The tallest on record is 78 in (198 cm) tall from its shoulder to its feet.

■ The smallest horse is the Falabella pony. These tiny horses grow to about 30 in (76 cm) from shoulder to feet.

■ Zebras have been bred with donkeys to make a light brown animal with very fine stripes called a zedonk.

■ Zebras and horses have one toe on each hoof, cattle and deer have two, and hippos and rhinos have three.

■ Racehorses are bred for speed and gallop at up to 45 mph (70 km/h).

Horse galloping

Q A Why are zebras black and white all over?

The truth is, no one knows. Some scientists believe that the pattern of stripes is like a fingerprint that helps zebras to recognize each other and keep the herd safely together. Others say that the stripes are there to dazzle predators (animals that hunt them) or even to keep zebras from getting too hot or cold.

Q A Why do camels have long legs?

Long legs help keep a camel's body as far away from the ground as possible. In the hot deserts where camels live, the air can be 18°F (10°C) cooler around a camel's body than it is around its feet. Long legs make them fast, too, and camels are ridden in races, where they run at speeds of about 20 mph (33 km/h).

Q A Which horses work the hardest?

Mules are used to carry heavy loads because they have the strength of a horse and the stamina (power to keep going) of a donkey. In fact, mules are half horse and half donkey—they always have a horse mother and a donkey father.

Camel

Q A What does a camel have in its hump?

Some people think that camels store water in their humps, but in fact they store food. A camel's hump is made of extra fat, which is slowly used up if the camel doesn't get enough to eat. As the fat is used up, the hump gets smaller.

Mule

Przewalski's horses

Q A Which horses are really wild?

Most horses live with humans, and only one truly wild type of horse is still alive today—Przewalski's horse. By the 1960s, even this was only found in zoos. Now, specially bred herds of Przewalski's horses are being put back onto the grasslands of Mongolia, to live in the wild again.

Can mammals swim?

Mammals live almost everywhere in the world, including in the ocean, and sea mammals are superb swimmers. Just like mammals on land, they breathe air and feed their young on milk, but instead of arms and legs, they have flippers or fins, and some have lost almost all of their fur. Whales, dolphins, porpoises, seals, and sea lions all have strong, streamlined bodies that cut through the water Some ocean mammals can swim underwater for up to 90 minutes without coming up for air.

Orca, or killer whale

Male orca is up to 30 ft (9 m) long and weighs up to 10 tons

• Sharp-toothed jaws attack everything from fish and squid to seals and whales

• Sky-white belly for camouflage from below

• Large, paddle-shaped flippers

How do walruses keep warm?

Walruses live and swim in freezing Arctic waters, but they don't have much fur to keep them warm. Instead, a walrus has a very thick layer of fat, or blubber, under its skin. On land, walruses huddle together in large groups for extra warmth. They can weigh up to 2¼ tons (2 metric tons), but they are strong swimmers and divers—they can dive more than 330 ft (100 m) deep and stay there for 25 minutes or more.

Male walrus with tusks removed

How does a whale breathe?

Whales breathe through large nostril flaps called blowholes on the tops of their heads. Most whales have one blowhole, but some have two. When a whale comes up for air, it opens its blowhole and snorts air out so fast that it sends up a huge spray. Then it breathes in deeply and closes its blowhole to dive again.

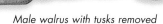

Orca about to dive, with blowhole closed

Orca coming up for air, with blowhole open

Which whale is the friendliest?

Dolphins are the most playful, curious, and friendly of all the whales. They live in groups, help each other hunt, and take care of each other—if a dolphin is sick or injured, another one will push it to the surface so it can breathe. Wild dolphins often seem to be interested in humans and will follow boats or swim with human divers. There are even stories of dolphins saving drowning people.

Bottlenose dolphin

Whiskers used to find food on seabed •

Front flippers used for balancing and turning •

Dugong

More Facts

■ Blue whales eat up to 6½ tons (6 metric tons) of tiny, shrimplike krill every day.

■ Baby blue whales drink more than 26 gallons (100 liters) of milk from their mothers every day for 6–8 months.

■ A blue whale's massive heart is the same size as a small car.

■ When a seal dives, its heart beats ten times more slowly than normal.

■ Dolphins make more than 300 click sounds per second and use the echoes of their clicks to find their way around.

Dolphin clicking

Which hunter has to watch its back?

Seals are talented undersea hunters, with streamlined bodies and powerful flippers that help them to chase fish—but they can end up as meals themselves. Polar bears stand beside ice holes and wait for seals to come up for air, then grab them. Killer whales smash into ice banks to knock seals into the sea, then eat them. Even sharks attack them. But the biggest threat is from humans, who hunt seals for their skin, fur, and blubber.

Fur seal

Which cows swim in the sea?

Dugongs. These odd-looking, gentle beasts are often called sea cows. Like cows, they have chubby bodies and large, square snouts, and they spend most of the day grazing on grass—but dugongs eat sea grass, which grows in shallow waters. Dugongs are the only vegetarian mammals in the sea. They often travel in herds, pulling up whole plants as they eat and leaving trails of bare seabed behind them. Instead of fleeing from sharks and other hunters, they sometimes gang together and head-butt them.

BIRDS

What are birds?

Birds are the biggest, strongest and fastest fliers of all animals. Their bodies are built for a life in the air. They have light skeletons, feathers instead of fur, and wings instead of arms or front legs. All birds can stand upright on their two back legs, have horny beaks for mouths, and lay eggs with hard shells.

Q **A** **Do birds use nutcrackers?**

Nut-eating birds use their beaks to crack nuts. Then they spit out the shell and swallow the nutmeat. Parrots are the only birds that hold nuts with their feet while cracking them. They also use their hooked beaks to scoop pulp out of fruit.

Red parrot

Young starling in flight

Long, uneven primary feathers along edge of wing provide lift

Bird feathers are oily to help keep them waterproof

Thin, strong beak for snatching insects or seeds

Softer down feathers keep the bird warm

Long tail feathers act as a rudder to help the bird steer in the air

Perching birds have long, thin toes to grip on to branches

How do birds fly?

Birds take off and fly in a way similar to airplanes, but birds do not have engines. They power themselves by flapping their wings. The wings push against the air in the way that a rowboat's oars push against water.

1 To begin its flight, this tawny eagle flings itself forward and raises its wings.

2 Its strong breast muscles pull the wings downward. This powerful stroke lifts the bird and moves it forward.

3 As the bird raises its wings again, the long primary feathers spread out so the wings can move through the air more easily.

4 The bird levels out. With each downstroke, the outer, primary feathers work hardest to lift the bird and push it forward. On the upstroke, the shorter, inner feathers help the bird stay high in the air.

Green hummingbird

Q A Which bird has the most feathers?

The swan has more than 25,000 feathers on its body. Small birds such as hummingbirds have around 900. Only birds have feathers, which are made from keratin, the same stuff that makes our hair and nails. Birds use their beaks as combs, preening their feathers daily to make sure they all lay flat and there are no insects hiding in them.

Woodpecker

Climbing birds have four toes

Q A Why do hummingbirds hum?

They don't hum as humans do—the humming sound is made by the birds' wings beating the air at up to 80 times a second. Hummingbirds hover in front of flowers to feed on nectar, the sugary liquid that bees also eat. Hummingbirds are the only birds that can fly backward.

Mute swan

Q A How many toes do birds have?

Most of the world's birds are perching birds—they rest on branches—so their toes are designed to grip. They have four toes—three at the front and one facing backward. Birds that climb, such as woodpeckers, also have four toes, but with two pointing forward and two backward. Some water birds have just three webbed toes, and others have three long toes in front for walking on sand or mud and a tiny raised toe at the back.

Q A Which birds dye their feathers?

Flamingos do. The pink coloring in the tiny pink shrimp and algae they eat dyes their feathers. These lanky birds live around salty lakes and rivers in South America, the Caribbean, and Africa. They stand in water and scoop up food with their bills upside down.

Greater flamingo

Long, bare legs for wading deep into water

Q A Which bird has the longest feathers?

The feathers in a peacock's fan can be up to 7 ft (2 m) long. These fabulous, brightly colored feathers aren't part of the peacock's tail—this is much shorter and is behind the fan. They are just for impressing the females—peahens have shorter, drab gray feathers.

Peacock holding up its fan

Are birds dangerous?

Birds of prey can be very dangerous to other birds, fish, or small mammals—these meat-eating birds are fierce hunters and kill for food. Birds of prey are strong fliers. They have clawed toes, called talons, for snatching and killing their prey, and sharp hooked beaks for tearing into its flesh. Birds of prey are the only birds that kill with their feet, and are often known as raptors, from the Latin word for "seize."

Q A Which birds go fishing?

Fish eagles hunt by swooping down on fish near the surface of the water and scooping them up in their curved talons. Their rough, scaly feet help the birds to keep hold of the slippery prey. Fish eagles live alongside seas, lakes, and rivers and include some of the biggest and most spectacular eagles, such as the American bald eagle.

Sea eagle feasting on salmon

• *Primary feathers fanned out to help bird brake rapidly*

• *Long, broad wings for soaring—wingspan can reach 6 ft (180 cm)*

Red-tailed buzzard with feet outstretched, ready to pounce on its prey

Q A Which birds have the best eyesight?

Birds of prey have terrific eyesight and detect prey from a great distance. A golden eagle can spot a rabbit at least 1 mile (1.6 km) away. Birds of prey have eyes that stare straight ahead, because their eyeballs are too large to swivel— they turn their heads to look to the side.

Tail spread out to slow the bird for landing •

More Facts

Sparrowhawk plucking a blackbird

■ Sparrowhawks can turn upside down in midair to catch other birds.

■ Many owls have one ear higher than the other. This helps them to pinpoint exactly where their noisy prey is.

■ The smallest birds of prey are the pygmy falcons. They can weigh just 1 oz (28 g) and be as short as 5½ in (14 cm).

■ The Andean condor has wings that stretch out to 10 ft (3 m) from tip to tip. It weighs up to 30 lb (13.5 kg).

■ The lanner falcon kills its prey by smacking into it with such great force that the prey sometimes falls dead to the ground.

Lanner falcon

• Talons lock onto prey and pierce the flesh

Q A ## Why do vultures have bald heads?

When a vulture feeds on a large animal, it pokes its head right inside the body. If the vulture had feathers on its head, they would get covered in blood, which is sticky and hard to wash off. Vultures are very clean birds. They always take a bath after a meal, if they can, and will fly long distances to find water.

Eagle owl

Q A ## How do owls hunt in the dark?

Owls can hunt in almost total darkness, and most prefer to venture out at night. All owls have excellent hearing. They can pick up the faintest rustling of voles or mice on the ground and pinpoint exactly where it is coming from. Then they swoop silently down on their prey, snatching it with their claws.

Q A ## Which bird of prey throws rocks?

The Egyptian vulture uses rocks as tools to crack open ostrich eggs. Ostrich eggs are the largest eggs in the world and have tough shells, but they make a fine meal for a small vulture. Egyptian vultures eat other birds' eggs, too—but because these eggs are smaller, they can pick them up and drop them on the ground until the shell smashes.

White-backed vulture

Secretary bird carrying a snake

Q A ## Which bird of prey kills by kicking?

The secretary bird uses its strong legs and feet to stamp its prey to death, often kicking a snake in the head with its back toe. This long-legged bird is 4 ft (1.2 m) tall. Despite its gangly size, the secretary bird can fly, although it hunts by stalking across the grasslands of Africa, often walking 15 miles (24 km) a day.

Egyptian vulture

What's in a nest?

Birds will make use of whatever they can find. As well as leaves, twigs, feathers, and bits of straw, bird nests can be made of mud, moss, animal hair, string, paper—or even bits of plastic bags. Nest-building is hard work, so some birds make nests they can use year after year—unless other birds find the nests and move in.

Q A Why don't some birds build nests?
Not all birds lay eggs in nests— some use tree holes or high ledges. In the icy Antarctic, King penguins take turns holding their eggs on their feet to keep them warm until they hatch.

King penguin with its egg

• Top of nest is made from small twigs and leaves

Q A Why do some birds feather their nests?
Birds use feathers to line their nests and make them warm and cozy. Usually, they collect old feathers dropped by other birds, but small birds sometimes grab them straight from bigger birds' backs.

Redstart nest

• Big twigs make a strong base

Kestrel chicks in a secondhand buzzard's nest

What's inside an egg?

Like all birds' eggs, this quail's egg is a perfect little survival capsule. Inside it is food, liquid, and a tiny speck of life called an embryo. As soon as the egg is laid, the embryo begins to develop into a chick. The growing chick feeds on the yolk sac until it is used up and the chick fills up most of the space inside the egg. It is ready to hatch...

1 The chick starts to hammer at the blunt end of the egg with its beak.

2 After lots of pecking and resting, it breaks a circle of eggshell away.

3 Within an hour of hatching, the chick's feathers are dry, and it can stand up.

More Facts

- Hummingbirds' eggs are often as tiny as your fingertip. The smallest of them is only ⅜ in (1 cm) from end to end.

- Emus lay eggs that change color. At first, the eggs are dull green, but after a few days they turn black.

Kiwi egg

Emu egg

- The biggest birds' eggs ever found weighed 26 lb (12 kg). They were laid by the elephant bird of Madagascar, which died out over 700 years ago.

Ostrich egg

- The largest egg today is the ostrich egg. Each egg is about 7 in (18 cm) long and can weigh up to 3¼ lb (1.5 kg).

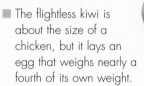

- The flightless kiwi is about the size of a chicken, but it lays an egg that weighs nearly a fourth of its own weight.

Elephant bird egg

- Some of the biggest nests are made by bald eagles. One old nest in Florida was 9½ ft (2.9 m) wide and 20 ft (6 m) deep.

- A male bowerbird builds a bower, or thick arch, to attract a female, and decorates it with colorful fruits and flowers, or even scraps of plastic.

- The song thrush completely lines the inside of its nest with mud. The mud waterproofs the nest so well that it keeps the rain out for months.

Waterproof nest

Do birds need lessons in nest-building?

Q / A No—birds are born knowing how to do it. They do get better with practice, though. Each type of bird builds its own kind of nest and cannot build any other.

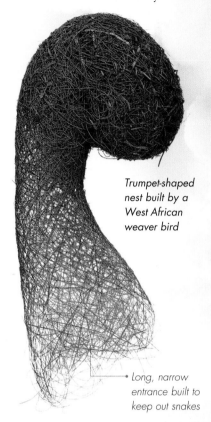

Trumpet-shaped nest built by a West African weaver bird

Long, narrow entrance built to keep out snakes

What do parents do when their eggs hatch?

Q / A They become feeding machines. The young of many small birds, such as blue tits, are completely helpless when they hatch. The only thing they can do is eat. The parents bring them food almost continuously for about three weeks, until the chicks are ready to leave the nest.

After 3 days, the chicks are 4 times bigger than when they hatched

Which birds have their babies adopted?

Q / A Cuckoos trick other birds into hatching and bringing up their young. Cuckoos lay their eggs one at a time in the nests of smaller birds. A cuckoo's egg is tiny for such a big bird, so the new parent is fooled into thinking the extra egg is one of its own and caring for it.

Cuckoo's egg

European robin's eggs

How do birds hide their eggs?

Q / A Some birds lay their eggs out in the open, on the ground or a rocky ledge, and need to protect them from hungry predators. The eggs are usually colored and patterned with streaks and splotches, since this helps them to blend in with the stones or rocks around them.

Three differently colored guillemot eggs

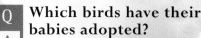

Blue tit chicks

REPTILES

AMPHIBIANS

How old are crocodiles?

These large reptiles were around when the dinosaurs ruled 65 million years ago, and they have not changed much since. Crocodiles and their relatives—alligators, caimans, and gavials—are among the oldest animals still alive on Earth. Most of them live in rivers and lakes and are powerful killing machines with long, strong tails, bony armor-plating, and mighty jaws with more than 60 sharp, pointed teeth.

American alligator

Q A When is a crocodile not a crocodile?
When it's an alligator. They are hard to tell apart—crocodiles have a pair of teeth that stick out over their top jaw, and alligators have wider, shorter snouts.

* *Powerful, flexible tail pushes the crocodile through water*

* *Nile crocodiles can grow to nearly 20 ft (6 m) in length*

* *Like all reptiles, crocodiles have tough, scaly skin*

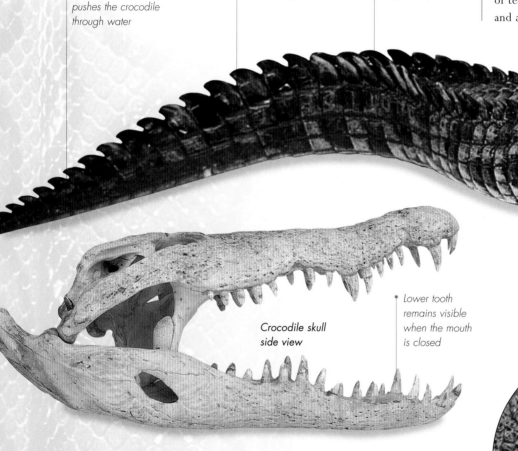

Crocodile skull side view

* *Lower tooth remains visible when the mouth is closed*

Edge of clear eyelid *Top eyelid* * *Bottom eyelid*

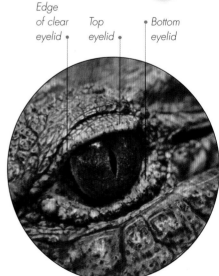

Crocodiles have three eyelids: a top one, a bottom one, and a clear lid to protect the eye underwater

Q A Do crocodiles lose their teeth?
Crocodiles are always losing their daggerlike teeth. They use them to grab their prey, drag it underwater, and hold it there until it drowns. As the victim struggles, it often pulls out a few of the crocodile's teeth, but new ones soon grow in their place.

Q A Do crocodiles cry?
Crocodiles' eyes have glands that make tears as our eyes do, but not because they are sad. Crocodiles cry when they have been on land for a while and their eyes are beginning to dry out. The tears clean their eyes and help their eyelids slide across smoothly.

Q A What is a gavial?

It's an odd-looking crocodilian with a long narrow snout. Only one type of gavial is alive today—it lives in the rivers of northern India. Gavials spend most of their lives in water, and their legs are so weak they can hardly walk. Gavials use their long jaws to snap up fish and birds, then swallow them headfirst.

Gavial skull

Q A How do caimans swim?

Like other crocodilians, caimans glide along with only their eyes and nostrils poking above the surface. This means a caiman can stay hidden until its unsuspecting prey comes close. Then, by flicking its long, strong tail, it surges through the water and grabs its meal.

Caiman with its eyes and nose above water

Nile crocodile

A crocodile may grow up to 50 sets of teeth in its lifetime

More Facts

■ The biggest alligator ever found was 19 ft (5.84 m) long, but most alligators grow to about 9¾ ft (3 m).

■ Crocodilians can't chew. They have to rip their food apart, tearing off bite-sized chunks of flesh to swallow whole.

■ Alligators are loyal mothers. They build huge nests and lay up to 60 eggs, then stay with their young for at least a year.

■ Female crocodiles scoop their young hatchlings into their large jaws and carry them from the nest to the water.

■ Crocodiles yawn, but not because they are bored or tired. Opening their jaws helps them to cool down quickly.

Tough, platelike scales protect the crocodile's belly

Clawed feet for clambering up slippery river banks

Q A How fast do caimans grow?

Like their alligator cousins, caimans take a long time to grow up. They are 8 or 10 years old before they are big enough to breed. When they hatch, caimans can be less than 8 in (20 cm) long, but the largest—the black caiman—can grow to 20 ft (6 m).

Young caiman

Nile crocodile

How do snakes eat?

Most snakes have jaws that can open so wide that they are able to gulp down an animal much fatter than themselves. Large snakes can even eat deer or small crocodiles. They do not chew—instead, they swallow their prey whole, headfirst so the legs slide down more easily. Snakes have long, slim bodies, no eardrums, poor eyesight, and no legs—yet they are among the world's deadliest hunters.

Model of a poisonous rattlesnake's mouth

Front fangs for injecting poison fold back when not in use •

• Venom glands make and store poison

Teeth often get stuck in their prey and are swallowed with the food •

Bottom jaw is divided in two halves and can stretch sideways •

Q A Which snakes are the most deadly?

Mambas, vipers, and cobras all have bites that are deadly to people. A bite from a king cobra will kill its prey in minutes as the poisonous venom paralyzes the victim's lungs and heart.

Cobra ready to strike

A tablespoon of dried cobra poison could kill 165 people •

Q A Are all snakes venomous?

No, although some harmless snakes pretend to be venomous. The milk snake doesn't have any venom, but it is patterned and colored to look like a deadly coral snake. The only difference is the order of the stripes—coral snake stripes are red, yellow, and black.

Milk snake

• Milk snake stripes are red, black, and yellow

How are snakes born?

Most baby snakes hatch from eggs. Snakes usually lay their eggs somewhere warm, damp, and sheltered, then leave them. The soft-shelled eggs swell in size as they soak up moisture from around them. Inside the egg, the young snake feeds on the yolk and grows for up to three months until it is fully formed. Its body is tightly coiled in the shell, and it is time to break out...

1 The young snake rips the shell with a small egg-tooth on the end of its snout.

2 It sticks out its head and tastes the air with its tongue to check if it is safe.

3 When the time is right, the baby snake will quickly slither out and hide.

More Facts

- Some snakes squeeze other animals to death. Boa constrictors coil their body around their prey. As the animal breathes out, the boa tightens its grip, until the prey suffocates.

- The smallest snakes are thread snakes. Some fully grown thread snakes are only around 4 in (10 cm) long.

- Green anacondas are the heaviest snakes. They can weigh 400 lb (180 kg)—as much as two men.

- The longest snakes are reticulated pythons. They live in the rainforests of southeast Asia, where they grow up to 33 ft (10 m) long.

Indian python

- As many as 1,000 rattlesnakes may gather in one den to keep warm.

- A grass snake will play dead when it's under attack. It lies with its head upside down and its tongue out, and gives off a terrible smell.

Grass snake pretending to be dead

Rat snake

- A large meal can keep a snake going for several weeks or even months.

Q A Can snakes climb trees?

Many snakes are agile climbers, especially snakes that live in swamps and rainforests. Mangrove snakes can grow longer than 6½ ft (2 m) and spend the day resting in a high branch. At night, they hunt for lizards and frogs or raid nests for birds.

Mangrove snake

Q A Why do snakes stick out their tongues?

By flicking out its forked tongue, a snake picks up tiny scent particles in the air. It tastes the air to track down food, find a mate, or sense an enemy.

Q A Do snakes have backbones?

Every snake has bones, but except for its skull, a snake's skeleton is just a backbone and ribs. The backbone is a long chain of many small bones called vertebrae.

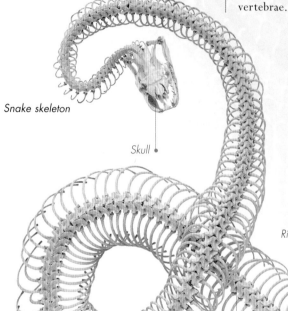

Snake skeleton

Skull

Rib

400 vertebrae

Q A Which snakes like eggs for breakfast?

Some snakes eat nothing but eggs, and only birds' eggs at that. An egg-eating snake will swallow an egg whole until it pushes against the neck bones and breaks. The contents of the egg are squeezed into the stomach, and the shell is pushed back out of the mouth.

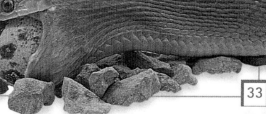

Egg-eating snake

How fast are lizards?

Many lizards can bolt in the blink of an eye. They need to be fast on their feet to escape from bigger animals who see them as tiny, tasty snacks. The racerunner lizard is the fastest reptile on land, reaching speeds of 18 mph (29 km/h)—a lot faster than most humans. Some reptiles don't need to be so speedy—tortoises and turtles carry protection with them.

Crested water dragon

• *When it's frightened, this lizard rears up and runs on two legs for extra speed*

• *Long tail used for support and balance*

Gecko's toe, spread out to get the best grip

Underside of a gecko

• *Strong back legs power the lizard forward*

5 toes with sharp claws for climbing

Blue-tongued lizard

Q A Which lizard has a shocking tongue?

The Australian blue-tongued lizard has a bright blue tongue. When it's under attack, the lizard opens its mouth and hisses, sticking out its startling tongue. This horrible sight is usually enough to scare its attacker away.

Q A Which lizard can walk up walls?

Geckos can run up walls and even across ceilings. They get their grip from soft, brushlike pads on the bottoms of their five toes. These pads are made of millions of tiny bristles that hook onto any bumps and cracks in the surface.

How do lizards escape?

Some lizards will try anything to escape from danger, even if it means leaving bits of their bodies behind. When threatened, the lizard waves its tail around to persuade the attacker to grab it. The small bones running down the length of the tail have tiny cracks in them, and when the tail is tugged, the bones separate and the tail breaks away. This gives the lizard a chance to flee.

1 *This tree skink has lost the end of its tail. The part that broke off will keep twitching for a few minutes to keep the attacker busy.*

2 *Two months later, the tail has begun to grow back. Growing a new tail takes a lot of energy and is hard to do if food is scarce.*

3 *After eight months, the tail is almost fully grown. It will be able to break again, but not in the same place.*

More Facts

- The Texas horned lizard defends itself from attack by squirting jets of toxic blood out of its eyes.

  - The largest lizard is the Komodo dragon. It grows up to 9¾ ft (3 m) long and can weigh more than two humans.

    - The scales on a lizard's skin are made of keratin, the same stuff as human fingernails.

  - Basilisk lizards can run across water on their back legs. As they slow down, they sink and have to swim the rest of the way.

Lizard scales

- The shingleback lizard looks as if it has two heads. Its large, stumpy tail confuses predators and lets it escape.

Shingleback lizard (head below)

- Galapagos giant tortoises can live for more than 100 years and reach 3 ft (1 m) in length.

Madagascan chameleon

Q A How can a lizard disappear?

Some lizards can change the color of their skin to blend in with the background. Most of them make their skin lighter or darker, but chameleons can change colors completely and make skin patterns appear and disappear. They don't only change colors to hide—an angry chameleon will go black with rage.

Male Jackson's chameleon flicking out its tongue

Q A Which lizard has the longest tongue?

A chameleon—its tongue is longer than its body. The chameleon keeps its tongue rolled up inside its mouth. When a tasty insect comes within range, the tongue shoots out and sticks to it. Then the tongue and the bug are reeled in.

Q A Which reptiles live in a box?

Tortoises and turtles do—their box is the thick shell covering their entire body, except for their head, tail and legs. When danger threatens, the turtle or tortoise pulls these soft parts inside and waits.

Hingeback tortoise

Q A What is a terrapin?

A terrapin is a type of turtle that lives in ponds and lakes, not the sea. Terrapins eat plants, worms, and insects. The terrapin known as the red-eared slider spends most of its life in the water, only leaving to bask on hot, sunny days.

Red-eared slider

Q A Which reptiles are the best swimmers?

Turtles are the champion reptile swimmers. Some large turtles can reach speeds of 18 mph (30 km/h), and many large turtles journey hundreds of miles in search of food or to lay their eggs.

Green turtle

Powerful front flippers pull the turtle through the water

Are amphibians wet?

Most amphibians, such as frogs and toads, are born in water and spend the first part of their lives in water, but then they move onto land as adults. Even as land-dwellers, they lose water very easily through their skin and have to keep their bodies wet. This is why they are most often found in damp places. Like reptiles, amphibians are cold-blooded, which means they need the warmth of the sun to give them energy to move.

European fire salamander

Salamanders and newts are the only amphibians that keep their long tails as adults

An amphibian's skin is soft and often slimy, and has no scales or hair

A bony ridge protects an amphibian's eyes

Salamanders have 4 legs and feet with 3 toes, but no claws

The fire salamander's bold colors warn other animals that it is poisonous to eat

Q A How many kinds of amphibians are there?

Salamanders, newts, frogs, and toads are all amphibians. There are also some odd, wormlike amphibians called caecilians. Caecilians have long, legless bodies, sharp teeth, and a special tentacle under each eye, which they use to smell their prey. Most live in rainforests, where they burrow into soft soil or leaf litter.

Caecilians can be anything from 3 in (8 cm) to 5 ft (1.5 m) long

Caecilian skeleton

Q A Which baby never grows up?

The axolotl is a salamander that spends its whole life in water. Most amphibians start as larvae and breathe through gills as fish do. Then they grow lungs and move onto land. Axolotls never lose their gills or become adults.

Q A What do toads carry on their back?

Male midwife toads are unusual because they carry eggs on their backs, sometimes from more than one mother. The female lays the eggs in strings, and the male wraps the strings around his legs. He carries them until they are ready to hatch, and then drops them into ponds or pools.

Eggs wrapped around the toad's legs

Male midwife toad

Q A What do salamanders eat?

All salamanders are carnivores—they eat other animals, mostly small, slow-moving ones such as slugs, snails, and worms. They usually creep up on their prey and make a quick grab. On land, some salamanders flick out their sticky tongues to snatch their victims. In water, they suck in their prey and grip it with their teeth.

Mandarin salamander eating an earthworm

Female great crested newt

Q A Can amphibians fly?

A Costa Rican flying tree frog appears to fly as it leaps from branch to branch high in the trees, but it doesn't have any wings. The webbing between the toes of the frog's feet spreads wide and acts like a parachute to slow the falling frog. This lets it glide farther so it can escape hungry predators.

European common toad, puffed up

Q A Who lays their eggs on a leaf?

A female newt swims underwater to lay one egg at a time on a water-plant leaf. Then she uses her feet to fold the leaf around the egg, which hides it and protects it from being eaten. Some newts will carefully lay between 200 and 400 eggs in this way, one by one.

More Facts

■ Poison-dart frogs are the smallest amphibians. Some are ¾ in (2 cm) long, about the size of a bumblebee.

■ The Surinam horned frog has a very big mouth and easily swallows rats or other frogs whole.

Surinam horned frog

■ Like lizards, some salamanders can shed their tails if threatened. The attacker goes after the wriggling tail, and the salamander escapes.

■ The Japanese giant salamander grows up to 4½ ft (1.4 m) long.

Q A Which toad blows itself up?

When it's under attack, the European common toad tries to look threatening by puffing up its body with air and standing up straight on all four legs. Other amphibians use different tricks to defend themselves. Some have poisonous skins, some change their skin color to hide, and some head-butt their attackers.

Legs spread out and used as paddles

California newt

Tail can be lashed from side to side to increase speed

Q A How do newts swim?

Newts like to take it easy when they swim. They puff air into their bodies to help them float, and stick their legs out like paddles to push themselves along gently. They can speed up if they need to, by paddling with their legs and lashing their tails from side to side to propel themselves through the water.

Are toads frogs?

Frogs and toads are not the same, but they are closely related. Nearly all frogs and toads have big, bulging eyes, wide mouths, long back legs, and boxy bodies. There are thousands of different types, too, and it can be very hard to tell them apart. Most toads have lumpier, drier skins than frogs. Most frogs have longer back legs and webbed feet, and they leap higher than toads. Toads often prefer to live on dry land and frogs near water—but not always.

European common frog leaping for a woodlouse

Q A What makes a frog leap?

Most frogs eat insects and will leap at any tasty morsel that comes their way, hoping to catch it with their long, sticky tongues. Leaping out of the way of predators is also the best way to avoid being eaten.

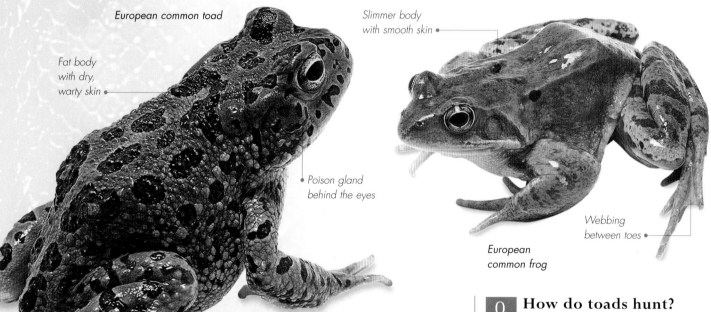

European common toad

Fat body with dry, warty skin •

• Poison gland behind the eyes

Slimmer body with smooth skin •

Webbing between toes •

European common frog

• Feet have very little webbing between the toes

Q A How do toads hunt?

Most toads don't hunt—they sit and wait for their food to pass by. When a tasty insect comes close, the toad sticks out its tongue or leans forward to grab its prey, then gulps it down whole.

How does a frog grow?

As a frog or toad grows from egg to adult, its body changes shape completely. This change is known as metamorphosis. The European common frog lays thousands of jellylike eggs in a thick, gloopy mass called frog spawn. Many eggs are snapped up by hungry fish, but the surviving eggs begin their incredible change as the little black specks start to turn into tadpoles.

1 The male frog hugs the female tightly as she lays up to 20,000 eggs.

2 After six days, the eggs hatch into tadpoles, with gills for breathing under water.

3 Nine weeks later, the tadpoles still have their tails, but they have grown legs and their gills have been replaced by lungs.

More Facts

- The male Darwin frog swallows his mate's eggs and keeps them in the vocal sac in his throat. The eggs hatch inside him, and the tadpoles jump out of his mouth.

- Glass frogs from South America look as if they are made from see-through jelly. From underneath you can see right inside their bodies.

- Tree frogs have sticky pads on the ends of their fingers and toes to help them climb.

Large, sticky pads

White's tree frog

Q A Can frogs climb trees?

Some tree frogs spend their entire lives in trees. They eat, sleep, and lay their eggs there. This red-eyed tree frog lays its eggs on leaves that hang over water. When the tadpoles hatch, they drop into the water below, grow into frogs, and then climb trees.

Red-eyed tree frog

Model of a marine (or cane) toad

Marine toads grow up to 9 in (23 cm) long

Cutaway shows inside the large poison gland

Poison can squirt up to 3 ft (1 m) away

Q A How big can frogs grow?

Bullfrogs can grow to more than 8 in (20 cm) long. The biggest of all is the Goliath bullfrog, which is 14 in (40 cm) long. The bullfrog is also one of the noisiest frogs. It makes a deep mating call from the large vocal sac under its throat.

African bullfrog

Extra-large vocal sac

Shrinking tail of froglet

4 The tail gradually shrinks until, by 16 weeks, it has disappeared. The new froglets are ready to leave the water.

Q A Why do toads taste terrible?

Toads taste like the poison that covers their skin. Some toads just taste horrible, but others are so poisonous they can kill—an animal that swallows a marine toad can die in 15 minutes. All toads have a large, lumpy poison gland behind each eye. When the toad is scared, the gland makes a liquid which oozes out onto its skin.

Toads have 4 toes on the front feet and 5 on the back

INSECTS

What is a butterfly?

Butterflies and moths are among the brightest and biggest insects in the world. Some tropical butterflies have a wingspan that is 13 in (32 cm) across. Like other insects, a butterfly's body has three parts (a head, a thorax, and an abdomen) and six pairs of legs. It also has two pairs of wings. There are more than 165,000 kinds of moths and butterflies, and all turn (or metamorphose) from crawling caterpillars into delicate fliers.

Zebra butterfly

False-eye moth

The lacewing's wingspan is 3½ in (9 cm)

Wings of moths and butterflies are covered with minute scales

Lacewing butterfly resting with wings folded together

Butterflies have tiny clubs at the ends of their antennae

Q A How can you tell a butterfly from a moth?
It's not always easy to spot the difference. Many butterflies have brighter colors and fly by day—moths tend to fly at night. When resting, butterflies fold their wings on their back—moths hold theirs out flat. Most moths have thicker bodies and feathery antennae.

Q A Why do butterflies and moths wear disguises?
Butterflies and moths don't have claws or fangs to defend themselves, so many have grown to look like leaves, bark, or rocks. This camouflage helps them to hide from birds, and stops them from becoming a tasty snack.

Indian leaf butterfly (top) sitting next to real leaves

How do butterflies grow?
There are four stages in the life cycle of a butterfly or moth.

1 Eggs are laid on their own or in groups, like these Blue Mormon butterfly eggs. A tiny caterpillar hatches from each egg and eats the shell.

More Facts

- Moths have an amazing sense of smell. Females give off a scent that is picked up on a male's feathery antennae several miles away.

- Butterflies and moths "taste" things with their feet. They lay their eggs on the tastiest leaves, so their caterpillars have the food they need to grow.

- The Asian vampire moth can pierce a cow's skin and drink its blood.

- Many moths don't eat or drink anything at all. An Indian moon moth only lives for a few days, just enough time to find a mate and lay eggs.

- The monarch is the longest-living butterfly of all. It can survive for a year.

- Darwin's hawk moth has the longest proboscis—12 in (30 cm)—to reach the nectar inside a long orchid flower.

Q/A How far can a butterfly fly?

Monarch butterflies can cover 80 miles (130 km) in just one day. Each fall, millions of them migrate (move to warmer lands). They fly from Canada in the far north and California in the west to Mexico in the south. In spring, they fly back—a total journey of up to 1,860 miles (3,000 km).

NORTH AMERICA

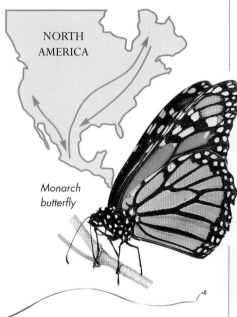

Monarch butterfly

Q/A What do butterflies and moths feed on?

Butterflies and moths have a liquid diet. They drink through a long hollow tube called a proboscis, and suck up nectar from flowers, juices from rotting fruit, and watery sap from trees. Some butterflies even slurp liquids that ooze from dead animals. When not in use, the proboscis is kept coiled under the head.

Proboscis is about 3 times the length of the moth's body

Darwin's hawk moth

Postman butterfly caterpillars

Passionflower vine

Q/A How do caterpillars keep themselves from being eaten?

Some caterpillars disguise themselves to look like the plants they feed on, but others have a more brutal trick. They eat poisonous plants and become poisonous themselves. Postman caterpillars, for instance, feed on poisonous passionflower vines without becoming ill—but if a bird eats the caterpillars, it gets very sick and quickly learns to leave them alone.

Q/A Why do caterpillars breathe through holes?

Insects do not have any lungs to help them breathe—instead, they take in air through tiny holes in the sides of their body. These are the open ends of tubes called spiracles, which carry air around the insect's body.

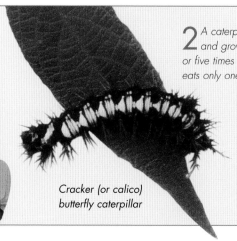

Cracker (or calico) butterfly caterpillar

2 A caterpillar's goal is to eat and grow—it sheds its skin four or five times as it grows. Each type eats only one particular plant.

3 When it has grown, a caterpillar turns into a pupa. A butterfly's pupa (or chrysalis) is usually hard, while most moths spin a soft silk cocoon. Inside, the caterpillar is changing.

4 Weeks later, the pupa splits open and out crawls the adult butterfly. Its wings are damp and crumpled—the butterfly lets them dry before flying off.

Blue morpho pupa and butterfly

Are beetles tough?

All beetles are covered with a form of armor-plating to protect their bodies. A beetle's top pair of wings is hard and leathery and forms a tough casing, which shields its delicate flight wings underneath. Many beetles also have hard coverings over their head and thorax, and some have large, clawlike jaws. Male beetles often get tough with each other—like most males in the animal kingdom, they fight over territory, food, or mates.

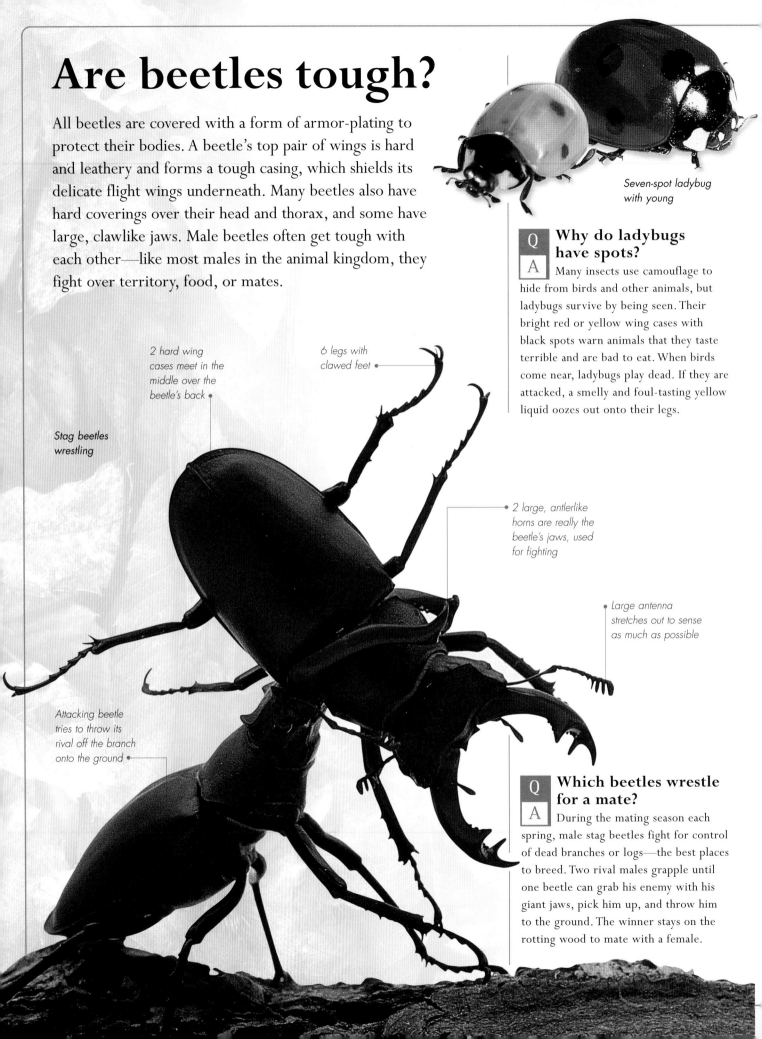

Seven-spot ladybug with young

Q A Why do ladybugs have spots?

Many insects use camouflage to hide from birds and other animals, but ladybugs survive by being seen. Their bright red or yellow wing cases with black spots warn animals that they taste terrible and are bad to eat. When birds come near, ladybugs play dead. If they are attacked, a smelly and foul-tasting yellow liquid oozes out onto their legs.

2 hard wing cases meet in the middle over the beetle's back

6 legs with clawed feet

Stag beetles wrestling

2 large, antlerlike horns are really the beetle's jaws, used for fighting

Large antenna stretches out to sense as much as possible

Attacking beetle tries to throw its rival off the branch onto the ground

Q A Which beetles wrestle for a mate?

During the mating season each spring, male stag beetles fight for control of dead branches or logs—the best places to breed. Two rival males grapple until one beetle can grab his enemy with his giant jaws, pick him up, and throw him to the ground. The winner stays on the rotting wood to mate with a female.

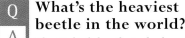

Which beetle is the enemy of potatoes?

Q A Colorado beetles are feared by farmers around the world because they eat the leaves of potato plants and can destroy whole potato fields. They breed rapidly, so they are hard to control. Each female Colorado beetle lays up to 2,500 eggs. The eggs take less than a month to hatch and grow into adult beetles, ready to start breeding.

Green tiger beetle

What's the heaviest beetle in the world?

Q A The Goliath beetle is the heaviest insect of all. It weighs about 3½ oz (100 g) and can grow up to 6 in (15 cm) long. If you put it on your hand, it would cover your palm. Goliath beetles live in Africa. They fly well for their size, and feed on fruit in trees.

Goliath beetle

Can beetles swim?

  Diving beetles can. They live in ponds and shallow lakes and are fierce hunters. They swim after tadpoles and small fish and also attack snails or other insects. They can't breathe under-water, but they carry air down with them, trapped beneath their wing case.

Scarab (dung) beetle

Which beetle is a killing machine?

Q A Tiger beetles have razor-sharp, curved jaws that they use for killing and cutting up insects. The larvae sit in small tunnels and stick their jaws out to grab passing prey. The adults spring out of sandy burrows to ambush their victims, chasing them at great speed—they can sprint as fast as a human can walk. When tiger beetles are attacked, they blast out a hot, smelly liquid that burns like acid.

Diving beetle

Which beetle likes to clean up?

Q A Dung beetles do—they can clear away an enormous pile of cattle dung in under 24 hours. They feed on it, but they also shape it into balls and roll it into their burrows. Then they lay their eggs in the dung so the young have something to feed on when they hatch. By recycling animal droppings, dung beetles help prevent diseases from spreading from piles of rotting dung.

How do beetles fly?

Most insects that can fly have two pairs of wings that fold back when they are not in use. Flying beetles can fold up their flight wings completely and hide them under their hardened wing cases. The wing cases are heavy and not much use for flying, but the powerful flight wings are strong enough to carry them. Some beetles can't fly if their muscles are too cold, so they need to warm themselves up first.

1 Before taking off, this cardinal beetle flaps its wings to warm them up. It tests the wind with its antennae.

2 When the beating wings reach flying speed, the beetle pushes its back legs and takes off.

3 The flight wings flap hard to drive the beetle through the air. The beetle holds its stiff wing cases still and out of the way of its beating flight wings.

Which insects sting?

Bees, wasps, and some ants sting—but only the females have a stinger. Some wasps use their stingers to attack prey, but bees and ants only sting to defend themselves or their hives or nests. When an insect stabs another animal with its stinger, it pumps poison into the wound, enough to hurt people and big animals and paralyze or kill small animals. Many flies bite, but they don't sting.

Q A Do wasps only sting humans?
Wasps will attack any animal that disturbs their nest—up to 100 wasps fly out to defend their home. Some wasps also sting other insects to paralyze them, then lay their eggs in or on them, so their larvae have something to eat when they hatch.

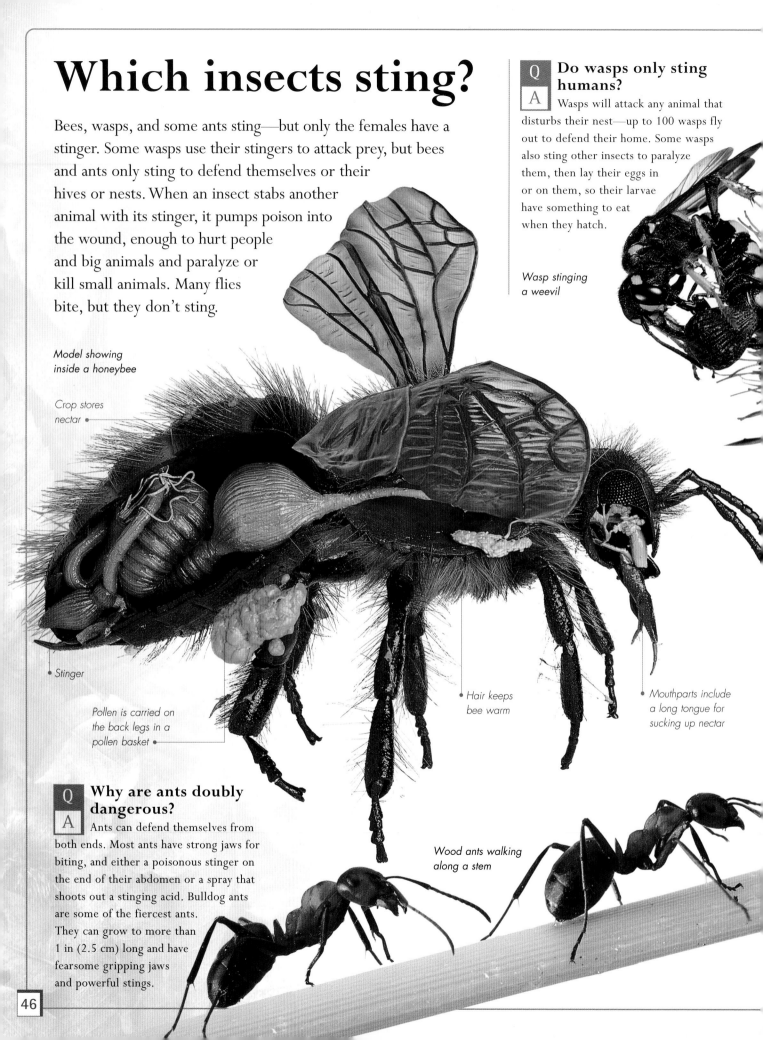

Wasp stinging a weevil

Model showing inside a honeybee

Crop stores nectar •

• Stinger

Pollen is carried on the back legs in a pollen basket •

• Hair keeps bee warm

• Mouthparts include a long tongue for sucking up nectar

Q A Why are ants doubly dangerous?
Ants can defend themselves from both ends. Most ants have strong jaws for biting, and either a poisonous stinger on the end of their abdomen or a spray that shoots out a stinging acid. Bulldog ants are some of the fiercest ants. They can grow to more than 1 in (2.5 cm) long and have fearsome gripping jaws and powerful stings.

Wood ants walking along a stem

Who works hardest in a beehive?

Worker bees do. Beehives are organized into three classes—queens, drones, and workers. The queen lays all the eggs, the drones' job is to mate with the queen, and the workers make honey, build the hive, and guard the queen.

Worker bees on a honeycomb

How do bees make honey?

They start by collecting nectar from flowers. The bees bring the nectar back to their hive or nest, where they store it in small wax cells called a honeycomb, to feed the hive. As the nectar dries out, it turns into a thicker syrup—honey.

How many times can a bee sting?

A bumblebee can sting as many times as it wants, but a honeybee can sting only once. This is because its stinger is barbed like a fishhook, so it stays in the wound when the bee flies away, and the bee dies. Only one honeybee can sting as often as she wants—the queen, who has a smooth, curved stinger.

Bumblebee collecting nectar

Which is the biggest wasp in the world?

The tarantula hawk wasp is the biggest. Its body is up to $3\frac{1}{4}$ in (8 cm) long, and its wings measure 5 in (12 cm) across. Tarantula hawk wasps don't often bother humans—they prefer spiders.

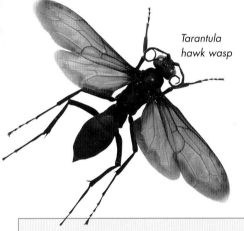

Tarantula hawk wasp

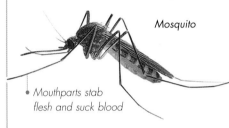

Mosquito

Mouthparts stab flesh and suck blood

Can flies kill people?

Mosquitoes are a type of fly, and in some countries they spread the disease malaria, which can be fatal. When a mosquito bites a person who already has malaria, it takes some of the germs with it. If the mosquito then bites another person, the germs are passed on into that person's blood, and they catch malaria.

How do wasps help humans?

Wasps kill lots of the caterpillars, grubs, and other small insects that feed on farmers' crops. However, the wasps don't eat the creatures they hunt. Most use them as living pantries for their eggs.

Do horseflies bite only horses?

No—female horseflies will attack any large mammal, so they bite cattle and people, too. The horsefly uses its knifelike jaws to make its victim bleed, and then it feeds on the blood. It even drools special saliva into the wound to stop it from healing. Male horseflies only drink nectar.

How does a wasp build its nest?

The nests are begun by a queen working on her own. The queen first creates a comb of four or five cells. She will lay one egg at the bottom of each cell. The nest is then built around this cell and is made from mud, wax, or chewed-up plant fibers.

1 A common wasp queen surrounds her comb with round paper walls made from chewed-up wood.

2 As the queen builds up the nest, she leaves just a small entrance, which is easier to defend.

View inside the nest, where the queen lays one egg in each cell

3 The first brood to hatch becomes workers and expands the nest. A big nest may be up to 18 in (45 cm) wide.

Are spiders insects?

No, spiders are not insects. They belong to a group of animals called arachnids. Unlike insects, arachnids have eight legs instead of six, and two body parts instead of three. All spiders are hunters and have a pair of fangs to inject venom into their prey and two short feelers called pedipalps. Most spiders have eight eyes, but some have only six.

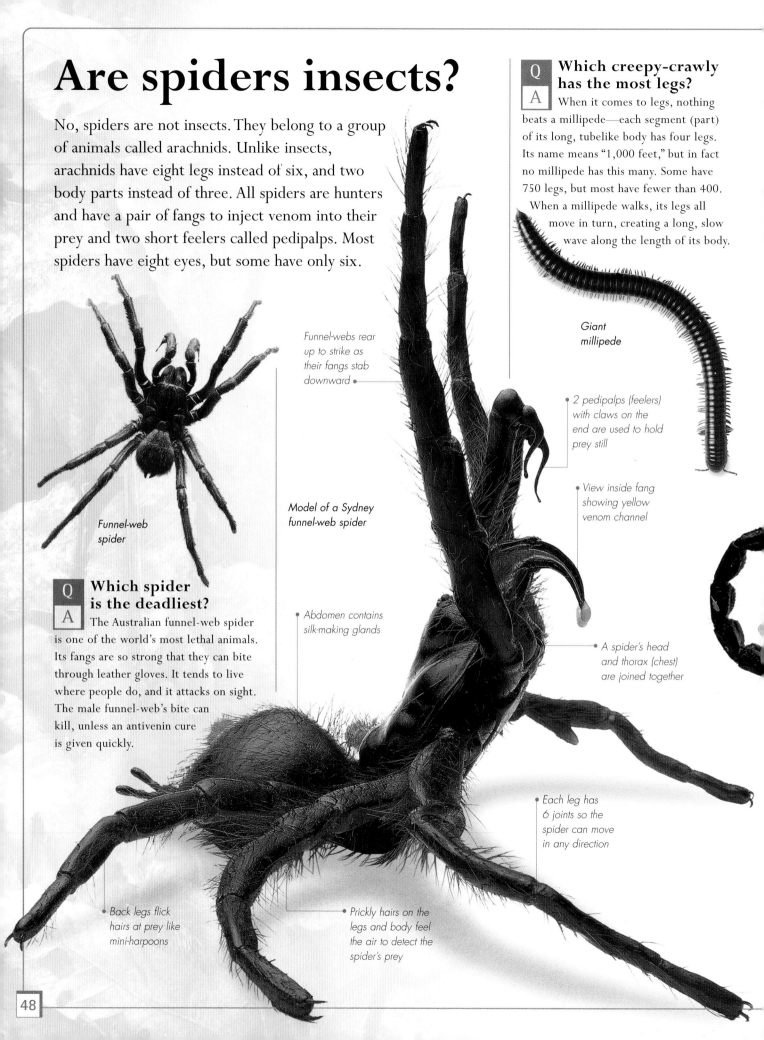

Funnel-web spider

Q A Which creepy-crawly has the most legs?

When it comes to legs, nothing beats a millipede—each segment (part) of its long, tubelike body has four legs. Its name means "1,000 feet," but in fact no millipede has this many. Some have 750 legs, but most have fewer than 400. When a millipede walks, its legs all move in turn, creating a long, slow wave along the length of its body.

Giant millipede

Funnel-webs rear up to strike as their fangs stab downward

2 pedipalps (feelers) with claws on the end are used to hold prey still

View inside fang showing yellow venom channel

Model of a Sydney funnel-web spider

Q A Which spider is the deadliest?

The Australian funnel-web spider is one of the world's most lethal animals. Its fangs are so strong that they can bite through leather gloves. It tends to live where people do, and it attacks on sight. The male funnel-web's bite can kill, unless an antivenin cure is given quickly.

Abdomen contains silk-making glands

A spider's head and thorax (chest) are joined together

Each leg has 6 joints so the spider can move in any direction

Back legs flick hairs at prey like mini-harpoons

Prickly hairs on the legs and body feel the air to detect the spider's prey

Black widow spider

Why are spiders scary?

Q / A Spiders are all killers, and although they rarely kill humans, they have a bad reputation. Most spiders have fangs that inject poison into their prey's bodies to paralyze them. The poison is usually harmless to us, but there are a few spiders whose bite is painful and deadly. The black widow is only 1½ in (4 cm) long, but its bite is 15 times more poisonous than a rattlesnake's.

• Female carries up to 30 babies for 2 weeks

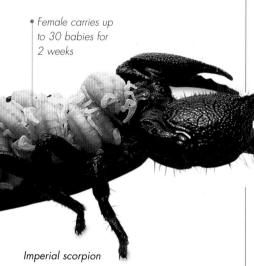

Imperial scorpion

Are scorpions caring mothers?

Q / A In some ways, the female scorpion is caring—but only up to a point. She carries her young around on her back after they are born. While they ride along with her, she will use her claws and stinger to defend them, but if any of them fall, off they are on their own. After the babies have shed their first skin and their new outer skin begins to harden, they climb down and scatter fast. On the ground, they risk being eaten—either by each other or by their own mother.

How many legs does a centipede have?

Q / A The name centipede means "100 feet," but these little creatures can have anything from 30 to 354 legs. The two front legs are in fact poisonous claws used to kill their prey. They eat mainly worms and insects, although some giant centipedes are 12 in (30 cm) long—big enough to eat mice and small frogs.

European centipede

How are scorpions like spiders?

Q / A Both are arachnids—they have eight legs and two body parts. Like spiders, scorpions have two clawed feelers called pedipalps, but a scorpion's pedipalps are huge, clawlike pincers for grabbing prey. Scorpions have another weapon that spiders don't have—a long, curved tail that ends in a poisonous stinger.

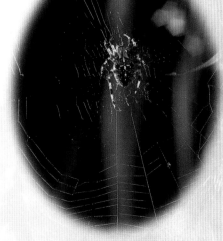

Orb-web spider

More Facts

■ Crab spiders hide in flowers and jump out to eat insects that land on them. Some change colors to match the plant.

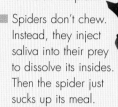

Crab spider

■ Spiders don't chew. Instead, they inject saliva into their prey to dissolve its insides. Then the spider just sucks up its meal.

■ Jumping spiders can leap up to 40 times their own length to catch their prey.

■ Tarantulas are spider giants—some have hairy bodies 4³⁄₄ in (12 cm) long and feed on birds or mice.

Mexican red-legged tarantula

How do spiders catch their prey?

Q / A Most spiders make silky threads and use them to build sticky webs, either round orb webs or messy silk traps on walls or on the ground. The webs look delicate, but the silk is strong enough to carry up to 4,000 times the spider's own weight. Insects blunder into the web and get stuck. Then the spider scuttles out and sinks its fangs into its victim.

FISH

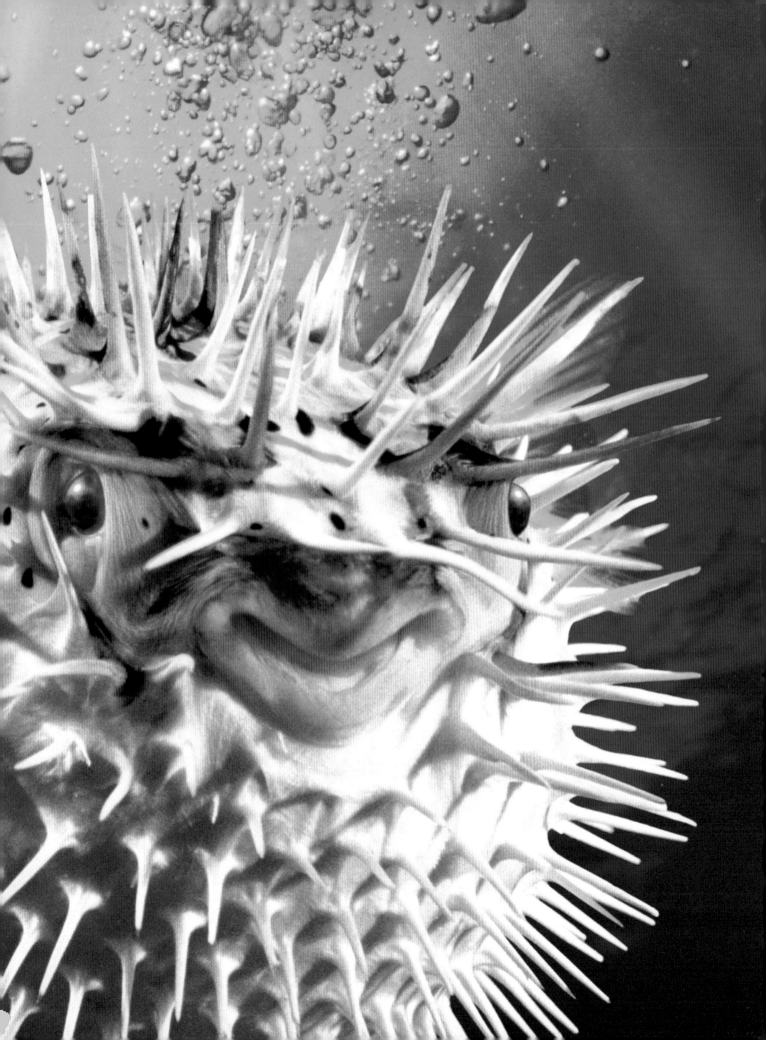

How do fish breathe?

All animals need to breathe oxygen, but unlike most animals, fish don't breathe air. Fish live underwater all the time, so they have to take their oxygen from the water around them, using special filters called gills. As the fish swims, water rushes into its mouth and through its gills. There, hundreds of tiny, leaflike folds take in oxygen, which goes into the fish's blood and around its body.

Q A Do all fish have bones?
All fish have skeletons inside their bodies, but not all of them are made from bone. Sharks, skates, and rays have skeletons made of cartilage—like the firm, flexible stuff in your nose. Most fish, though, have bone skeletons, so they are known as bony fish.

Cutaway model of an Atlantic cod

Muscles push tail from side to side

Smooth scales help fish slide through water

Bony backbone

Gas-filled swim bladder keeps fish level

Heart pumps blood around the body

Gills collect oxygen from the water

Twinspot wrasse

Q A Why do young fish swim in schools?
It is safer for fish to swim together in large groups (called schools or shoals) because they can confuse predators. There are so many small fish swirling around in a school that the attacker is dazzled and does not know which fish to attack.

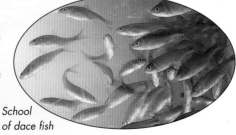
School of dace fish

Q A Why are some fish so colorful?
Many fish are multicolored to help them hide from their enemies. This wrasse has two large spots, like eyes, on its side. The "eyes" can fool hunters into thinking the wrasse is just part of a much bigger fish, and much too big to attack.

How do fish swim?

Fish swim in the same way that snakes wriggle—in an S-shaped wave that travels all along the body. Bundles of muscles on each side of the fish's backbone move, one after the other, to make the wave. It begins with a small sideways flick of the head and ends with a big swish of the tail, and takes about a second from start to finish.

This lesser spotted dogfish starts an S-shaped wave by swinging its head slightly to the right.

The wave begins to travel back along the body.

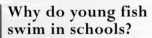
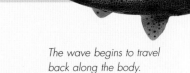

Q A What makes the lionfish so scary?

The sharp, deadly spines of the lionfish make it scary. Its bright colors and stripes warn other creatures that it is one of the most poisonous fish. Its venom can even kill a human. It swims among rocks and coral reefs in the warm seas of the Pacific and Indian oceans.

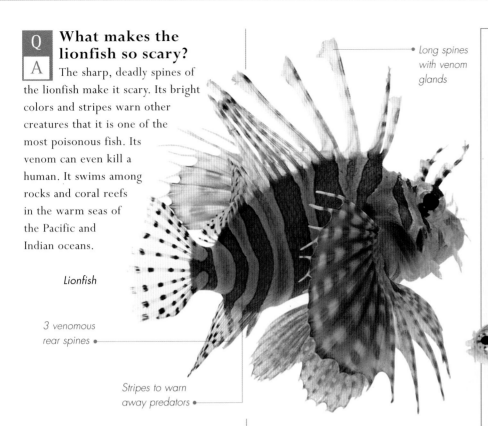

Lionfish

Long spines with venom glands

3 venomous rear spines •

Stripes to warn away predators •

More Facts

■ There are more than 24,000 species of fish in the world.

■ When they are scared, porcupine fish can swell up to two or three times their normal size by gulping in water.

Inflated porcupine fish

Deflated porcupine fish, with spines lying flat along its body

■ Fish have no eyelids.

■ The biggest fish is a whale shark. It can grow up to 45 ft (14 m) long.

■ Ribbon eels can measure up to 10 ft (3 m) long.

Q A Do fish make good parents?

Many fish scatter their eggs, then swim away and leave them. However, some parents are more protective. After a female bullhead lays her eggs, the male guards them for up to a month until they hatch. While he waits, he uses his broad fins to fan fresh water over the eggs—this keeps them healthy.

Wolf fish

Male bullhead

Q A Which fish snacks on shells?

Wolf fish grow up to 5 ft (1.5 m) long and have large, strong teeth. They use them for crunching through the shells of crabs, mussels, and other shellfish to reach the meat inside. This rapidly wears down the wolf fish's teeth, but new teeth soon grow to replace the old ones.

Ribbon eel

As the movement reaches the middle of the fish's body, the S-wave gets bigger.

The peak of the wave is now between the two back fins, and the tail is about to snap back.

The tail throws off the wave with a powerful flick to the right, while the head begins another wave.

Do all sharks bite?

Some of the biggest sharks, such as basking and whale sharks, do not even have any teeth. Instead, their mouths work like sieves, filtering bits of food from the water. Of the sharks that do have teeth, most are content to munch on other fish, and do not bite humans unless they are provoked.

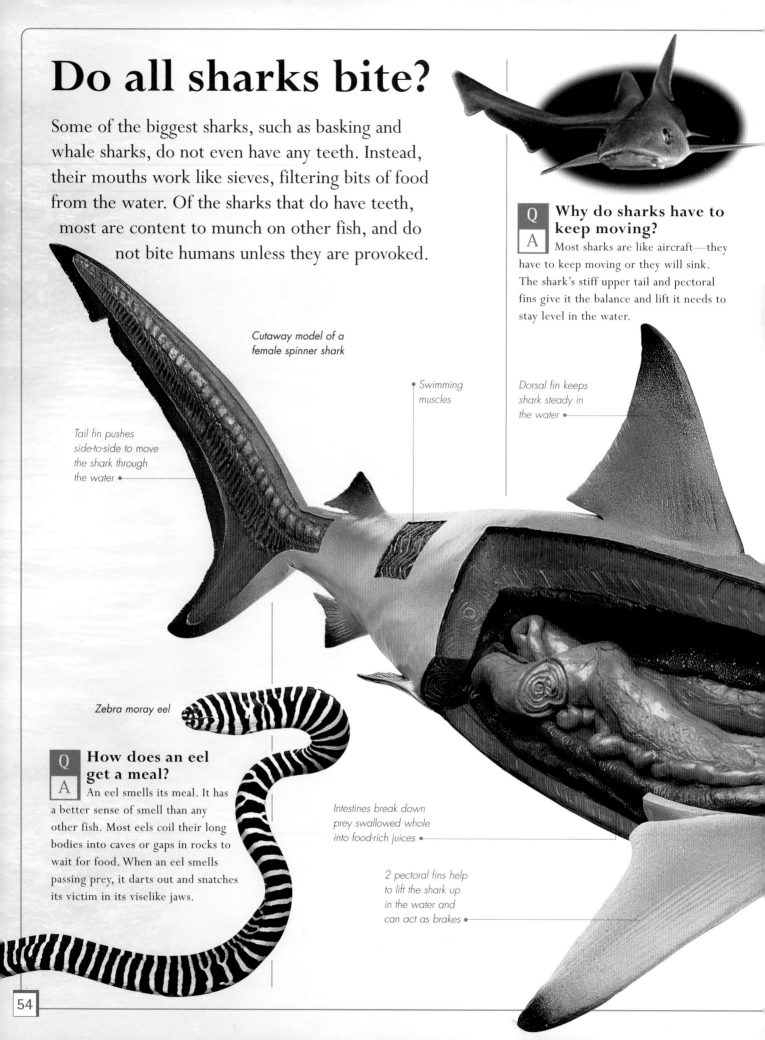

Cutaway model of a female spinner shark

Q A **Why do sharks have to keep moving?**
Most sharks are like aircraft—they have to keep moving or they will sink. The shark's stiff upper tail and pectoral fins give it the balance and lift it needs to stay level in the water.

Swimming muscles •

Dorsal fin keeps shark steady in the water •

Tail fin pushes side-to-side to move the shark through the water •

Zebra moray eel

Q A **How does an eel get a meal?**
An eel smells its meal. It has a better sense of smell than any other fish. Most eels coil their long bodies into caves or gaps in rocks to wait for food. When an eel smells passing prey, it darts out and snatches its victim in its viselike jaws.

Intestines break down prey swallowed whole into food-rich juices •

2 pectoral fins help to lift the shark up in the water and can act as brakes •

More Facts

■ The eyes of the hammerhead shark are at the ends of its wide head. A hammerhead swings its head from side to side as it swims to give it an all-around view of the sea.

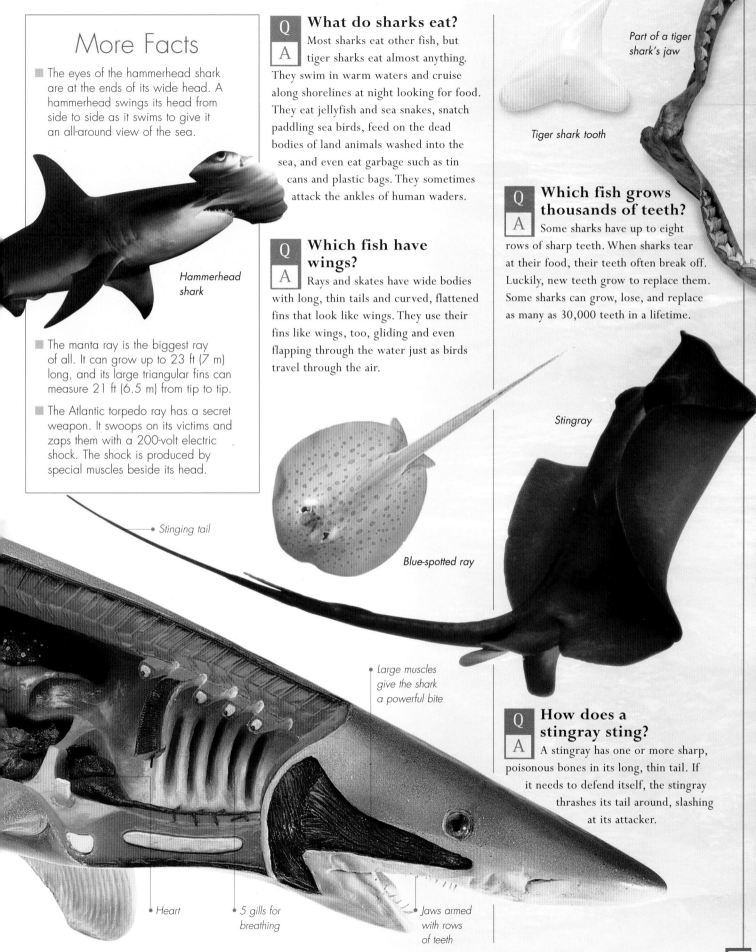

Hammerhead shark

■ The manta ray is the biggest ray of all. It can grow up to 23 ft (7 m) long, and its large triangular fins can measure 21 ft (6.5 m) from tip to tip.

■ The Atlantic torpedo ray has a secret weapon. It swoops on its victims and zaps them with a 200-volt electric shock. The shock is produced by special muscles beside its head.

Q A What do sharks eat?

Most sharks eat other fish, but tiger sharks eat almost anything. They swim in warm waters and cruise along shorelines at night looking for food. They eat jellyfish and sea snakes, snatch paddling sea birds, feed on the dead bodies of land animals washed into the sea, and even eat garbage such as tin cans and plastic bags. They sometimes attack the ankles of human waders.

Q A Which fish have wings?

Rays and skates have wide bodies with long, thin tails and curved, flattened fins that look like wings. They use their fins like wings, too, gliding and even flapping through the water just as birds travel through the air.

Stinging tail

Blue-spotted ray

Tiger shark tooth

Part of a tiger shark's jaw

Q A Which fish grows thousands of teeth?

Some sharks have up to eight rows of sharp teeth. When sharks tear at their food, their teeth often break off. Luckily, new teeth grow to replace them. Some sharks can grow, lose, and replace as many as 30,000 teeth in a lifetime.

Stingray

Large muscles give the shark a powerful bite

Q A How does a stingray sting?

A stingray has one or more sharp, poisonous bones in its long, thin tail. If it needs to defend itself, the stingray thrashes its tail around, slashing at its attacker.

Heart

5 gills for breathing

Jaws armed with rows of teeth

Do lobsters hide?

Lobsters are not really hiding in their shells, but they are protected by them. Lobsters, crabs, and other crustaceans living in the sea or in fresh water have hard, crusty shells to protect their soft bodies from head to toe—just like a suit of armor. The shell is an outside skeleton, and it is jointed so that the animal can move. When the animal outgrows its shell, it sheds it and grows another, larger one.

Q **Do any insects live in the sea?**

A No, but their distant cousins do. Crustaceans are creatures that have a hard shell and include animals such as crabs, shrimps, lobsters, and even woodlice. They belong to a group of animals known as arthropods, which also includes all the insects and spiders.

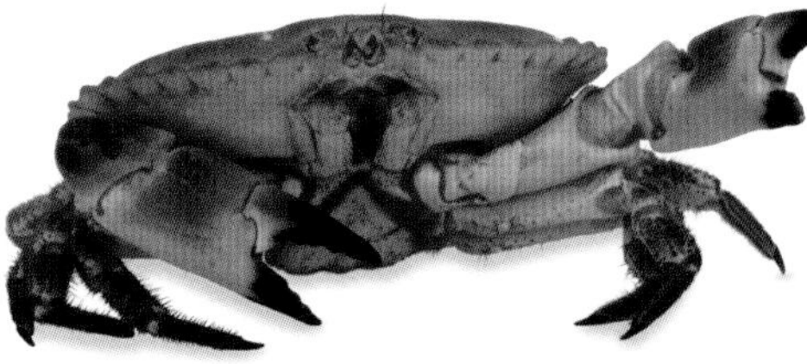

Common crab

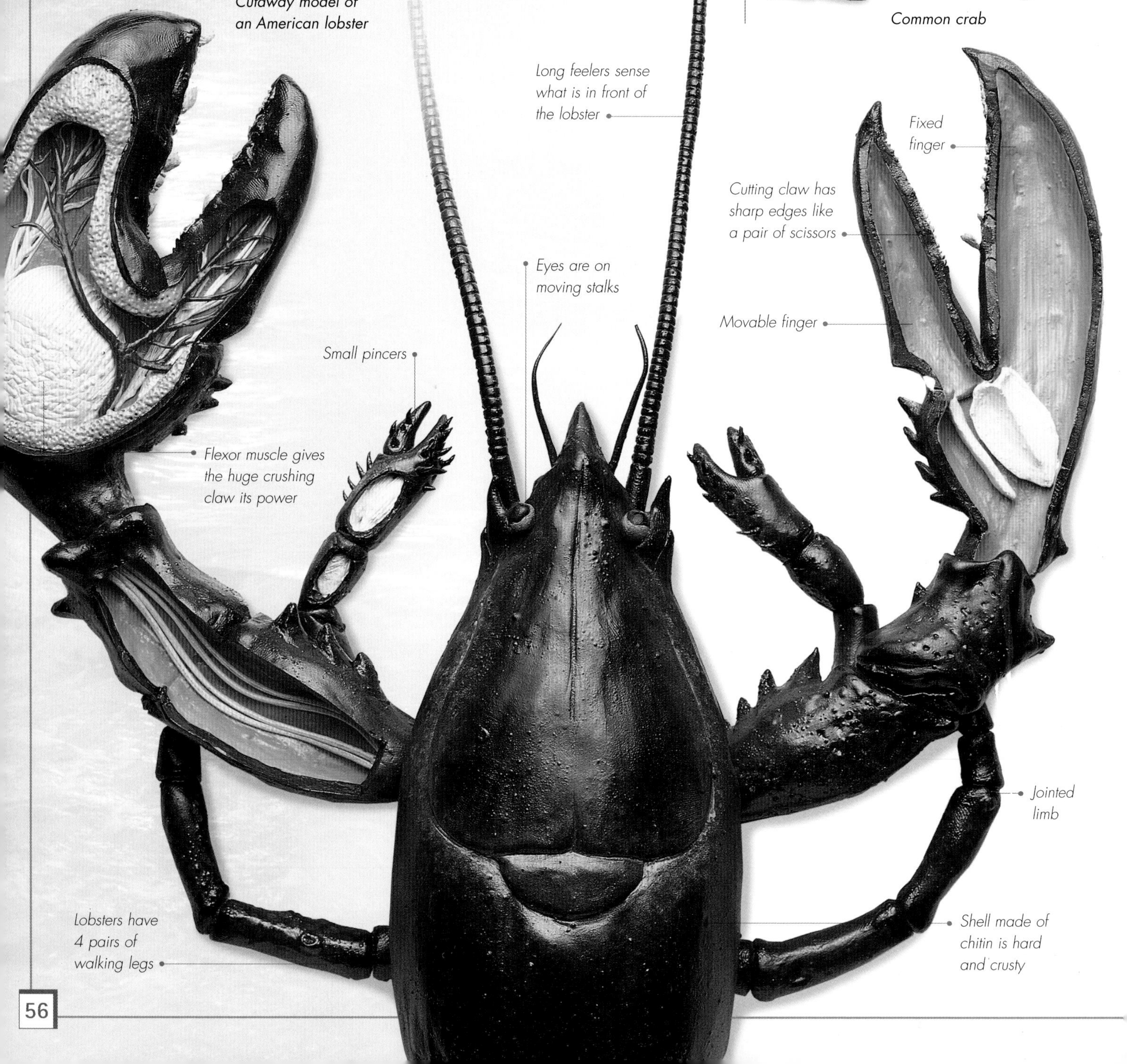

Cutaway model of an American lobster

Long feelers sense what is in front of the lobster

Fixed finger

Cutting claw has sharp edges like a pair of scissors

Eyes are on moving stalks

Movable finger

Small pincers

Flexor muscle gives the huge crushing claw its power

Jointed limb

Lobsters have 4 pairs of walking legs

Shell made of chitin is hard and crusty

56

Blue-ringed octopus

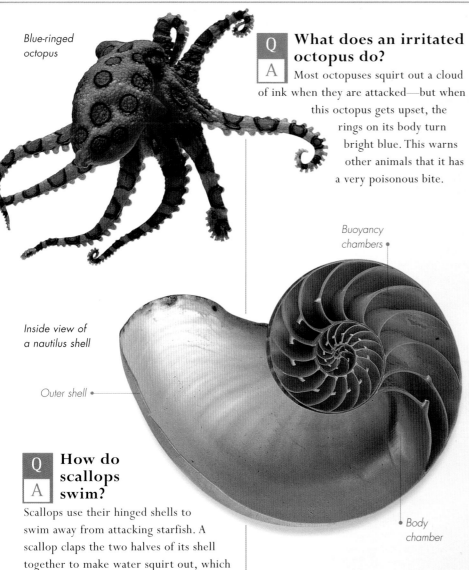

Q A What does an irritated octopus do?

Most octopuses squirt out a cloud of ink when they are attacked—but when this octopus gets upset, the rings on its body turn bright blue. This warns other animals that it has a very poisonous bite.

Buoyancy chambers

Inside view of a nautilus shell

Outer shell

Body chamber

Q A How do scallops swim?

Scallops use their hinged shells to swim away from attacking starfish. A scallop claps the two halves of its shell together to make water squirt out, which jets it out of danger.

Queen scallop

Eyes look like black dots

Q A Which snails eat meat?

The dog whelk is a flesh-eating sea snail. It creeps over rocks to feed on other shelled animals, such as mussels and limpets. The whelk pushes a hollow tube between the gaps in the animal's shell and scrapes out the creature's flesh with its sharp tongue.

Q A How does a nautilus float?

The squidlike nautilus has a shell filled with gas that makes it buoyant (float in the water). The nautilus lives in just the outer chamber of its coiled shell. As it grows, it keeps adding new buoyancy chambers to its shell.

Dog whelk crawling over a sponge on a rock

More Facts

■ Giant squid can grow to more than 65 ft (20 m) long—but they have never been found alive. Old sailors' tales of sea monsters were probably based on these oversized beasts.

Byssus

New Zealand mussel

■ Mussels spin a fine, strong thread called byssus (beard), which sticks to almost anything. They use their beards to grip on to rocks.

■ The giant clam can grow to more than 3 ft (1 m) across and weigh more than 440 lb (200 kg)—that's as heavy as a Shetland pony.

Decorator crab

■ The decorator crab dresses up in bits of seaweed, shells, and anything else it can find to camouflage its thin, spiny body on the ocean floor.

■ A hermit crab searches for empty shells to live in. When it grows too big for its shell, it leaves home and finds a bigger shell.

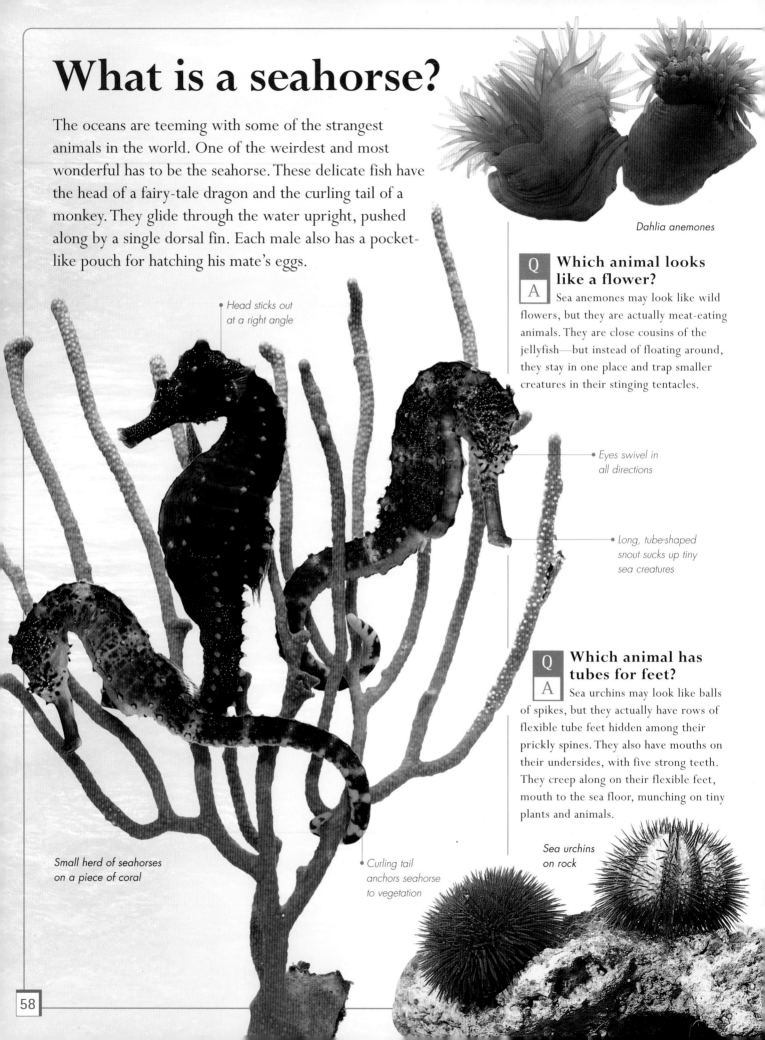

What is a seahorse?

The oceans are teeming with some of the strangest animals in the world. One of the weirdest and most wonderful has to be the seahorse. These delicate fish have the head of a fairy-tale dragon and the curling tail of a monkey. They glide through the water upright, pushed along by a single dorsal fin. Each male also has a pocket-like pouch for hatching his mate's eggs.

Dahlia anemones

Q A Which animal looks like a flower?
Sea anemones may look like wild flowers, but they are actually meat-eating animals. They are close cousins of the jellyfish—but instead of floating around, they stay in one place and trap smaller creatures in their stinging tentacles.

Head sticks out at a right angle

Eyes swivel in all directions

Long, tube-shaped snout sucks up tiny sea creatures

Q A Which animal has tubes for feet?
Sea urchins may look like balls of spikes, but they actually have rows of flexible tube feet hidden among their prickly spines. They also have mouths on their undersides, with five strong teeth. They creep along on their flexible feet, mouth to the sea floor, munching on tiny plants and animals.

Sea urchins on rock

Small herd of seahorses on a piece of coral

Curling tail anchors seahorse to vegetation

More Facts

- Pearls come from shellfish called oysters. When a piece of grit gets inside an oyster's shell, the oyster coats it until it is a smooth ball.

- The most expensive egg dish in the world is made from the eggs of sturgeon fish. It's called caviar, and one small spoonful can cost more than a thousand chicken eggs.

Black caviar

- The sea anemone's sting is deadly to most small animals, but not to the clown fish. This brightly colored fish lives among the anemone's tentacles, feeding off any leftover food caught by the anemone.

Seaweeds growing on a limpet shell

- Limpets spend the day creeping over rocks, scraping up tiny bits of food with their tongues. They return to the same place on the rocks every night— but no one knows how they find it.

- The box jellyfish can sting a human swimmer to death in four minutes.·

- The boldly striped zebra pipefish is very easy to see—until it hides behind water plants, lining its stripes up with their stems. Then it's almost invisible.

Zebra pipefish

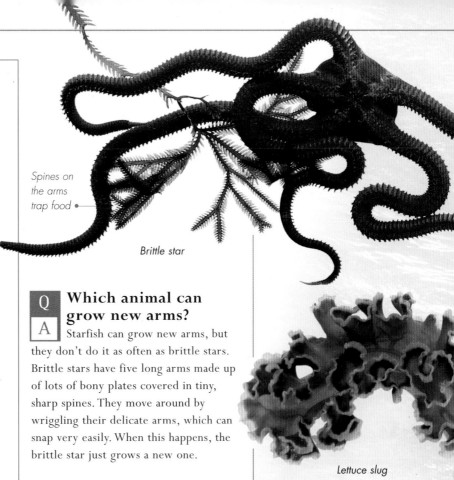

Spines on the arms trap food

Brittle star

Q A Which animal can grow new arms?

Starfish can grow new arms, but they don't do it as often as brittle stars. Brittle stars have five long arms made up of lots of bony plates covered in tiny, sharp spines. They move around by wriggling their delicate arms, which can snap very easily. When this happens, the brittle star just grows a new one.

Sea cucumber on a rock

Q A Which cucumber sucks up mud?

A sea cucumber has a bunch of sticky tentacles around its mouth, and it uses them to scoop up mud. It feeds on tiny pieces of food inside the mud and spits out the rest. It can pull the tentacles into its mouth to wipe them clean.

Lettuce slug

Q A Can you eat a sea slug?

This lettuce slug looks like a salad, but you wouldn't want to eat it— it's a cousin of the garden slug. It eats tiny, seaweedlike algae, which make it turn green. Since sea slugs have no shell to protect them, most of them are brightly colored to disguise themselves, or to warn enemies that they are bad to eat.

Q A Can fish walk on land?

Some fish can haul themselves onto land, but they can't go very far. Mudskippers often come up at low tide to feed on insects. They use their stubby pectoral fins like legs to push themselves along, and they breathe air through special gills filled with water.

Mudskipper

INDEX

The publisher would like to thank the following for their kind permission to reproduce their photographs:

a-above; b-below; c-center; l-left; r-right; t-top.

2-3 Getty: Digital Vision. 8-9 Getty Images: Gary Radall. 10 Jerry Young: 11bl ESPL/Denoyer Geppert: br University College: 14bc Ardea London Ltd: Jean-Paul Ferrero 15b Ardea London Ltd: Ferrero Labat 17cl Philip Dowell: 20-21c Getty Images: G.K & Vikki Hart. 26 Natural History Museum: 27crb Natural History Museum: 28-29tl, tr, c, cr, bl, br Getty Images: Art Wolfe. 31 Jerry Young: 32tr Jerry Young: 34tr, br Natural History Museum: 35t Jerry Young: 37tr Jerry Young: 39tr N.H.P.A.: Anthony Bannister 40-41c Getty Images: Inc. Luis Castaneda. 43 Jerry Young: 45c Natural History Museum: 47cr Natural History Museum: 49cl, bc Oxford Scientific Films: 50-51cl Getty Images: Steven Hunt. 55 Alamy.com: Douglas David Seifert 62-63tl Getty: Digital Vision.